Michel Remery
Ilse Spruit

Tweeting with GOD Manual

Exploring the Catholic
Faith Together

IGNATIUS PRESS   SAN FRANCISCO

Find #TwGOD on social media:

Download the TwGOD app!

Find more information about every page in this book using the free #TwGOD app.

- Download the #TwGOD app: www.tweetingwithgod.com.
- Use the app to scan any illustration with the scan logo.
- Watch videos, follow links, and read more, directly on your smartphone.

2.8 What is a 'nuncio'?

Tweeting with GOD Manual: Exploring the Catholic Faith Together

© 2015 by Michel Remery and JP2 Stichting, Leiden—www.jp2.nl

www.tweetingwithgod.com

Published 2015 by Ignatius Press, San Francisco
All rights reserved
ISBN: 978-1-62164-105-6
Printed in the United States of America

Table of Contents

Part A
Questions
about #TwGOD

Introduction

You may be a group leader or a teacher and still have many questions about the Catholic faith. You may feel you still have much to learn about your relationship with Jesus and still have much progress to make in following him. Yet, you want to share your faith with others and to respond to Jesus' call to "preach the gospel to the whole creation" (Mk. 16:15). You want to grow closer to God with others who want to do the same.

Whatever your background, your immediate question with regard to speaking about the faith may be: "How can I ...?" (1 Chr. 13:12). Like Moses, I am afraid (see Tweet 1.24); like Mary, I do not understand (see Tweet 4.5). I fear the questions of the people around me or of the young people in my group, and I am afraid I cannot answer them correctly (see A.6). This is a very human reaction. But based on my experiences of sharing the faith, I can assure you that God will provide everything you need.

This assurance is well founded. First of all, we have Jesus' promise: "Do not worry about how you are to defend yourselves or what you are to say; for the Holy Spirit will teach you at that very hour what you ought to say" (Lk. 12:11–12). At the same time, we are always called to collaborate with the grace of God (see Tweet 4.12). For our part, we can prepare ourselves by learning more about the faith. *Tweeting with GOD* can help us to do so.

As you grow in knowledge about our faith, you will discover more and more how everything is connected to God's love for us. Just stop reading for a moment and look at Jesus on the cross! What you see does not make sense unless you start to recognize its connection to God's plan of salvation (see Tweets 1.27 and 2.11). This is what I mean when I say that we intend to demonstrate the logic of the faith. It is logical because it is founded on God's love for us. In addition, there are many concrete and convincing arguments for the teachings of the Church, whether they concern Catholic doctrines, Christian ethics, or the spiritual life.

We do not claim to have all wisdom. This manual describes our method for sharing the faith, which works for us and which seems to work for the many people who are using *Tweeting with GOD* around the world. Just look at the way we started the project (see A.1): you can do the same! And you can do better, for hopefully you can learn from our mistakes!

Father Michel Remery

Tweeting with GOD (abbreviated as #TwGOD) started with the questions young people asked Fr. Michel Remery in his parish in the Netherlands as he greeted people after Mass on Sunday. Soon they came with so many questions that it was impossible to answer all of them with care. Fr. Michel invited them to send him their questions, and they did: they sent nearly 1,000 questions by Twitter, e-mail, Facebook, and scratches of paper. These messages gave rise to the title *Tweeting with GOD*, and the questions with their respective answers were called Tweets. After grouping the questions by topic and weeding out the duplicates, we started having regular evening sessions about the questions with a group of young people. In the beginning we agreed on some general rules so that our discussions would be respectful and fruitful (SEE A.2). These sessions, dedicated to St. John Paul II (SEE TWEET 2.50), continued for several years.

Format

The format of the discussions was always the same. We started with a brief opening prayer, led by one of the young people. Then we would take up one question and start debating about it. Often we needed the entire evening for one or two questions, as light was shed from many different angles. Often we needed to break down large questions into several smaller ones in order to investigate a topic in depth (SEE B.2 AND B.5). The brief summaries at the end of the session made reference to arguments supporting the teachings of the Church, based on the Bible, the *Catechism of the Catholic Church*, and other sources. These summaries later would form the basis of the book *Tweeting with GOD* (SEE C.1). The sessions were always concluded in the chapel, where we prayed the night prayer of the Church, Compline (SEE TWEET 3.13).

"Now I know where I stand in my faith"

Rowy: When I was seventeen I began to wonder what the faith was actually all about. At the #TwGOD sessions we could ask anything, and there was also room for discussion. It wasn't like we listened and had to accept everything we were told: what helped me a lot was that, through discussion and asking questions, we were able to find out what the Church believes. I could ask all the questions I had, no matter how critical they were. As a group we set out to find the answers. It was very important for me then, and it still is, to ask these questions. #TwGOD made me understand better what I truly believe in. Thanks to #TwGOD I have been able to strengthen my faith in Jesus, God, and the Church, and I now know better where I stand in my faith, which I try to live every day.

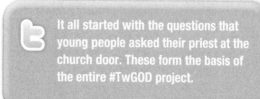

Effect

We could see the effects of our sessions. Participants would seek Fr. Michel after Mass: "Father, yesterday in the pub we continued the discussion, but I could not explain everything to my non-Catholic friend here. So we need to see you for a follow-up." Or they would invite their priest to the pub, into their circle of friends, with the request to dialogue about some questions that interested them. It was very moving to hear the news that a member of the group, which was open to everyone, decided to be baptized (SEE TWEET 3.36). At least one of them found her vocation to the religious life. Sometimes we had very personal discussions about sexual matters or difficult choices in life. Step by step, members of the group discovered how the teaching of the Church could help them even with these issues (SEE TWEETS 4.19–4.25).

Think, pray, act

The same strengthening effect can be observed among the members of the #TwGOD team today. We work hard together, speak regularly about the aims of our project, and also take time for prayer and for helping our neighbor, especially those who are marginalized. That way, we remind ourselves that knowledge of God does not suffice: our faith should always be expressed in our daily lives and in our personal relationship with Jesus.

> It all started with the questions that young people asked their priest at the church door. These form the basis of the entire #TwGOD project.

A.2 Why are questions at the heart of every #TwGOD activity?

Questions from people living in today's ever more secularized society form the basis of *Tweeting with GOD*. These questions are the expression of what we may call a budding thinking. Although in our modern world we hear opinions all around us, there are not many people who actually think carefully for themselves. Because at #TwGOD we consider individual thinking to be essential for understanding the faith and for integrating it into our lives, we have always encouraged questions of every sort, even when at first these might seem to be aggressive or disrespectful.

Often, a conversation began with opinions and critical questions the young people had heard elsewhere. But as we discussed possible answers, the further questions were more the result of their own thinking. Usually, the initial aggressive or insulting tone disappeared and was replaced with a genuine interest in pondering a topic more deeply. The background of that initial hostility may well have been insecurity or the fear of not being taken seriously. These experiences form the basis of the "rules" of #TwGOD (SEE BOX: 1 AND 5).

Ask, think, and learn

It is considered polite for a younger person to listen respectfully to an older person's opinions before speaking out himself. Without any judgment from our side, it must be observed that today this is no longer the attitude of many people. People often begin conversations not by listening but by presenting their own opinions. However, an open dialogue is possible only in an environment where people are really prepared to listen to each other. Only in that way is it possible to share honestly and also to learn from each other. Learning from others is not a matter of replacing our opinions with theirs but of moving beyond opinions toward the truth of things, which we discover by carefully listening to, probing, and thinking about the reasons behind people's statements. That brings us to rule 2 of #TwGOD (SEE BOX).

> **The "rules" of #TwGOD**
>
> 1. Welcome all questions regarding faith and life, regardless of the position they may represent or the answer they may imply.
> 2. Listen respectfully to the others in the group and try to understand the reasoning behind their statements.
> 3. Let the argumentation of the teaching of the Church speak for itself.
> 4. Do not try too hard to convince; simply testify to your own faith. Remember that only God can convert people's hearts.
> 5. Be discreet: don't blab about the statements of others to people outside the group.

SCAN

And the Church?

You may note that thus far we have not yet spoken of the teachings of the Church. That is because we intend to start where people are, with their lives and with their concerns. Every teacher knows that it is essential to attract the attention of his students before he can get his message across. Although we do not always wish to admit it, we are especially interested in subjects that are related to ourselves and our own lives.

The reason we only now come to speak of the teachings of the Church is that we strongly believe that they are true and reasonable. It is possible to give many arguments and reasons for faith. Logic is an important tool of #TwGOD (see Box: 3). But that is not all: the ultimate reasons for the Church's teachings are found not in earthly logic but in God's love for mankind. Ultimately, it is only in the light of God's love for the world and for us that answers to questions about faith can be formulated.

Not my responsibility

That brings us to a further conviction we have: I am not responsible for the conversion of people. Not ultimately, that is. I can and must collaborate, explain, proclaim, and testify, but in the end it is not I who converts the hearts of people: that is the work of God (see Box: 4; Tweet 4.50).

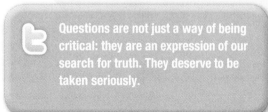

Questions are not just a way of being critical: they are an expression of our search for truth. They deserve to be taken seriously.

Questions call for answers. But who is entitled to give answers in a society where all opinions are considered equally valid? (SEE A.2). How can you possibly maintain that there is only one Truth, when there are so many convictions? (SEE TWEET 1.8). We are convinced that the answer to these questions can be found only in the person of Jesus, who invites each person on this earth to engage in a loving relationship with him.

Whose authority?

Today's world often seems to have an aversion to any authority where our minds are concerned: "I form my opinion, and you can hold on to yours!" Knowing this, in Tweeting with GOD we avoid as much as possible phrases such as "you must" or "you should." This aversion is not new: "By what authority are you doing these things?" (MK. 11:28), the crowd asked Jesus. Jesus does not start by judging and condemning: he starts by visiting the poor and healing the sick, whether their condition is physical or spiritual (SEE BOX). He even sits at the table of well-known sinners (LK. 5:29). Jesus starts where people are to be found. He visits them and talks to them about their concerns. His main "tool" to convince people is his love for them. That is what drives him, and that is what people find so attractive in him. And then, when a relationship has been established, Jesus goes further and explains all that is demanded to live life to the full.

Today's poor

Fr. Michel: Although unfortunately there are still many people who are financially poor, there is another poverty that does at least equal damage to human dignity. I have had some very uplifting experiences when celebrating the liturgy in small villages in Brazil, Suriname, and Tanzania, spending extremely joyful hours in the midst of people who had less than nothing. What a difference between their collective joy when celebrating Mass and the almost grim atmosphere in certain so-called more developed places, where I experienced a true spiritual poverty.

In our secularized world, with its shift toward the individual person, too often the collective experience of joyful celebration is lost. Partying then becomes a search for personal satisfaction. The problem is that this satisfaction can never be found solely in ourselves. The Christian message, by its nature communal, can change this grim atmosphere into real joy—not only because of what each receives but because of what each can share: love. Those who do not know this joy are to be counted among the poorest of the poor. Hence the great need of evangelization! (SEE C.6).

SCAN

God wants to share his love with us

The approach of *Tweeting with GOD* is based on this. We too intend to start where people are, with their questions, with their ailments, whether spiritual or physical. By witnessing to our own faith in Jesus, without imposing it on others, we demonstrate how to walk with Jesus. We invite others to get to know Jesus better by recognizing the logic of his teaching in the light of God's entire creation. We intend to demonstrate how every answer fits into the great plan of salvation that God has prepared for one reason only: to share his love with us.

More than dos and don'ts

Ultimately, the answer to faith-related questions is found not in logic or in the authority of the Church, but in a person: the person of Jesus, who loves each of us with a love we cannot truly imagine. That is why it is so important to help people to get to know Jesus before speaking about conditions or commandments. Any married couple can tell you about what they give up for each other, but they do so happily because of the love they share (SEE TWEET 4.19). But who would like to enter into a lifelong contract with an unknown person, only on the basis of a list of dos and don'ts? Only when they are growing into a personal bond with Jesus will people be able to embrace the rules of life he gives, knowing that these will help them to become truly happy as persons created by God.

> God's ultimate answer is his love for every person, expressed by the sacrifice of Jesus on the cross. There starts every answer.

Questions about #TwGOD

It is essentially human to ask questions. The beginning of philosophy is man's wondering about his experience in the world around him and asking questions. Down through the ages, men and women have asked the same questions: Where do I come from? Is there a purpose to my life? Is there life beyond what I can see? Why is there evil and suffering? How can I find happiness? God's revelation gives answers to these questions or at least helps us to make sense of them, even if we cannot know the fullness of truth until the life to come in the world to come (SEE TWEET 1.11).

#Today's questions

In our experience, most faith-related questions posed by people today are connected to these primordial questions. If you look closely at the 200 questions in #TwGOD, you will find that some questions are of the fundamental kind mentioned above (SEE #TwGOD, PARTS 1 AND 4). Others are about the nature of God and his creation, including the beginning and the end, and God's revelation to us in the Bible and in the Tradition of the Church (SEE #TwGOD, PART 1). Other questions are about Jesus and the institution of the Church (SEE #TwGOD, PART 2). Or they are concerned with prayer, liturgy, and the sacraments (SEE #TwGOD, PART 3). Finally, there are questions about how to live as a Christian (SEE #TwGOD, PART 4).

#Time and place

People in different times and places might phrase them differently, but the vast majority of the questions in #TwGOD are relevant not only to Dutch young people in the twenty-first century but to anyone living in any time or any place who seeks to understand the important things in life. Today, the #TwGOD program is used on different continents. The way in which the answers have been formulated is necessarily linked to place and time. An experience that many countries have in common is the

---

God's questions in the Bible

Have you ever searched in your Bible for the questions posed by *God*? They may differ slightly between translations, because Hebrew does not use punctuation.

God's first question is posed to Adam and Eve: "Where are you?" (GEN. 3:9), and it is directed to each of us! God comes looking for us because, like Adam and Eve, we have been tricked into disobeying him, and feeling bad about that, we have tried to hide from the truth. God's second question is to Cain: "Where is Abel your brother?" Cain, who has murdered his brother, answers with a question: "Am I my brother's keeper?" (GEN. 4:9). Again we are all addressed: we are indeed responsible for our brothers and sisters. We are to do good and not evil, and that includes helping each other to obey God.

In the New Testament, the first question is posed by the Magi, who, representing the entire world, inquire in our name about Jesus: "Where is he?" (LK. 2:2). This is where we begin Tweeting with God!

influence of secularization in different degrees. The answers of #TwGOD have been written from this perspective.

The vocabulary of #TwGOD is very modern, using as much as possible the language of our time. In a few decades, the text may be difficult to understand, as media such as Twitter and Facebook will have ceased to exist. The content of #TwGOD will be the same then, but it might need to be presented in a different way to answer the demands of that time.

For all generations

We can conclude that the questions of today's young people in *Tweeting with GOD* are universal questions, posed by every generation and every age. Therefore, it should not be surprising that even older people have said that they have been greatly helped by the simple and clear explanations in #TwGOD. (Some are even grateful for having been introduced to modern social media!) Thus, we will continue to engage in a dialogue about essential questions of people today, speaking in a youthful language about the eternal love of Jesus Christ for everyone.

 In spite of many differences, all people carry within themselves the same fundamental questions of their existence, the world, and God.

A.5 Can I use #TwGOD both alone and in a group?

The #TwGOD book can be used alone (see Box) as a reference or for study. It is also very useful for a single discussion session or a series of sessions. As people get to know each other as a group and are encouraged to think, it is possible for them to enter more deeply into the serious questions regarding our faith (see B.3). Thus it is useful to meet every week or two. For starters, we recommend that you review the outline of the original #TwGOD sessions (see A.1) and our suggestion for the format of a typical session (see B.2).

Ask and think

Whether you are alone or in a group, the starting point for every #TwGOD activity should be the questions you or your group have regarding the faith (see B.3). You will find that many of these questions will be directly answered by or at least related to the 200 questions in the book. As you think about possible answers, many more questions will arise, either directly connected to the topic concerned or on a completely different topic.

The aim of #TwGOD is to help people recognize the logic of our faith (see A.3). To discover this, it is indispensable for participants to think for themselves. Some people will simply repeat with a certain stubbornness what they have heard, without being able to give an explanation of what they believe (see A.2). Others will argue their point, but their arguments will be unfounded. That is not such a problem, though; we hope that they will learn to think for themselves as time goes by. No one has a prepared answer to everything!

The answers in the book *Tweeting with GOD* and on the website will facilitate both further study and dialogue about each topic. After group discussions, these answers will also serve as a reference when the discussion goes on outside of the sessions, as often will be the case (see A.1).

Using #TwGOD alone

Tweeting with GOD offers many ways in which you can search for answers to your questions. You can pick up a copy of the #TwGOD book or start browsing the app or the website: www.tweetingwithgod. com (see C.1). The book's index will help you to find quickly the Tweet in which the topic you are looking for is discussed. Furthermore, the website has a powerful search engine, also accessible through the #TwGOD app.

When you finish reading the answer to the question you searched for, you may wish to look up the scriptural quotations in your Bible or check out the "Read more" sections by using the app.

The aim is to grow in your relationship with God. That is possible only if you allow your growing knowledge about him to become part of your life. We invite you to make time for prayer every day and to practice your growing faith by helping others.

SCAN

Pray

It is very good and important to speak about the faith and to study it. Speaking about and studying the faith do not make sense, however, unless they are rooted in a (budding) personal relationship with Jesus. Hence it is fundamental to have regular moments of prayer. Also when you use #TwGOD in a group, prayer should be considered an integral part of the meetings. If you find that people are tired after the long discussions in the group and want to go home before the prayer, you may wish to shorten the discussions to make more time for prayer. Praying is literally Tweeting with God in that it gives you the opportunity to talk to him (SEE TWEET 3.2).

Act

It is essential that intellectual knowledge of God become part of your life and the way you treat other people. Jesus himself said that a tree can be recognized by its fruits (LK. 6:44) and a Christian should be recognized by the way he lives. The question "How does this affect my life?" is a very important one for everyone working with #TwGOD. When you use the program in a group, every session should address this question at some point.

It can be very helpful in this regard to do works of mercy, that is, to help people around you without expecting anything in return. You can do these alone or with your group.

> #TwGOD is about your questions, so start with these! The program can help you to find answers and to begin Tweeting with God yourself.

It can be awkward and painful to be approached about your faith by a friend who says, "Don't be silly! You can't possibly believe this religious nonsense!" It can be similarly distressing to be asked by someone in your discussion group, "Really? You don't believe this?" This may be even more the case when you are leading the group and realize that you do not have the answer to a straightforward question. Young people especially can be undiplomatically direct in their questions and comments.

Be yourself

How should you react in these cases? There is not a single way that works always and everywhere. You will need to find your own way of answering difficult questions without unthinkingly reciting answers given by others. Only then will you be both authentic and trustworthy. What helps a lot is to learn more about your faith, to read good books, and to talk to knowledgeable people. The #TwGOD answers should be able to give you a good start in every discussion.

"I did not want to be different from my nonbelieving friends"

Lidwine: At the time of the original #TwGOD sessions I was going through puberty. During that time the opinion of your friends and your relationship with them is very important. At school I had a group of friends who never spoke about faith or profound issues. Though I felt a desire to speak about those things, I didn't want to be different from my friends, and I was prepared to do anything to fit in with the group. Preaching by a priest can be good, but for me it definitely wasn't enough to make me explore the faith. It was a very big step from living my life with my friends from school, a life not compatible with the faith, to learning about the faith and living in accordance with the rules of the Church.

During the #TwGOD sessions I was able to learn about the faith and nonsuperficial stuff, together with people my own age. This was a good combination for me. I felt pushed by society in a direction that was not in sync with the Church, but I now experienced that it was in fact possible to be "normal" and religious at the same time. In the #TwGOD group I always felt safe. It was a place where I could plainly state what I believed and how I believed. I was allowed to ask tough questions without their being discarded as too critical. #TwGOD helped me a lot. I learned not to be afraid of hard questions posed by the people around me.

SCAN

Pray it away

In this context, as in every moment, prayer is essential. If you want to know more about your faith, get to know God! He has the answer to everything, although it is impossible to know the mind of God completely in this life. Based on your studies and your searching for God in prayer, you will start to see the great logic of our faith (SEE TWEETS 1.26–1.28). This logic will help you a lot as you search for the right answer. When you consider a difficult question in the light of God's love, you will find that you know more than you thought.

Do not fear

There is no reason to be afraid of questions, even when you do not know the answers. Nobody knows everything. We have a promise from Jesus himself that when we are questioned about the faith, the Holy Spirit will provide an answer (LK. 12:11–12). Of course, we have to open ourselves to the grace of God (SEE TWEET 4.12) so that we can hear his inspiration.

"Seek God first"

Ilse: I have learned not to trust only myself and my own knowledge. Only when I let God speak through me are young people interested in what I have to say. This means that I first have to work on my personal bond with God and regularly seek him in my prayer.

> Be authentic, pray, study, see the logic of the faith, and dare not to know. If you trust in God, you have no reason to be afraid!

Part B
Using #TwGOD in your group or school

Introduction

There are many ways in which you can work with *Tweeting with GOD*, and also many places: in the parish, at school, in a group preparing to receive a sacrament, and so forth. In the following chapters we give you an outline of how #TwGOD can be used fruitfully, based on our experience.

Feel free to adapt the suggested methods to your own approach, preferably working together with your group. The interactive methods we present will probably need to be adapted to the age and the composition of your group.

Note that the age of the group does not matter: #TwGOD is for all ages! We have observed that the youthful origin of #TwGOD (see A.4) makes the program's language accessible not only to young people, but also to more mature people who are seeking to learn about the faith. Not age, but the interest in learning more about the faith and questioning your own convictions forms the essence of #TwGOD.

In the following pages we frequently refer to the appendices in this manual, which give you a plan for a season with #TwGOD (see Appendix 1), some ways to encourage the group to ask questions (see Appendix 2), a number of interactive methods to use with your group (see Appendix 3), and ways to integrate the Sacrament of Reconciliation and prayer into the sessions (see Appendices 4 and 5) and to use #TwGOD with your Confirmation class (see Appendix 6).

We also prepared related downloads, with suggestions and interactive methods, that can be found at www.tweetingwithgod.com/howto. In addition, from time to time we will prepare for your group meeting a special, fully developed program on a specific topic.

You will also find in this manual an important section with advice for group leaders (see B.5). Through my own experiences as a youth leader, I have learned that a leader must first of all be a servant: someone who has the best intentions for his group and who is willing to make sacrifices, for example, in terms of time and energy, for that group. As you help young people on their faith walk, you will learn lessons that may sometimes be hard to accept yet are essential for your spiritual growth and that of those you meet! "[W]hoever would be great among you must be your servant" (Mt. 20:26).

Ilse Spruit

B.1 How do I start working with #TwGOD?

A useful way to start working with *Tweeting with GOD* is to have a chat with some people from the target group, to get to know their needs regarding questions about the faith. Often it will also work the other way around: some people talk about their questions regarding the faith and start wondering how to find answers to them. #TwGOD has both the answers to the questions and the method for helping people to think about the logic behind them.

#Team

After you have decided to start a #TwGOD group, it is a good idea to bring together a few people to form a team. One advantage of working in a team is that the target group can be represented in the preparations. Furthermore, by working in a team, you can divide the work, bring together more talents, and have a larger network from which to invite people to join the group. Team members can motivate each other and pray together. Last but not least, it is more fun to work together!

Share your vision

When you are planning a #TwGOD session, it is important to understand what you are trying to accomplish. Hopefully this is related to growing in your personal relationship with Jesus and learning more about God (SEE A.3). In addition to seeking answers to your own questions, you probably intend to help others to think about the faith too.

The "rules" of #TwGOD

1. Welcome all questions regarding faith and life, regardless of the position they may represent or the answer they may imply.
2. Listen respectfully to the others in the group and try to understand the reasoning behind their statements.
3. Let the argumentation of the teaching of the Church speak for itself.
4. Do not try too much to convince; simply testify to your own faith. Remember that only God can convert people's hearts.
5. Be discrete: don't blab about the statements of others to people outside the group.

(SEE A.2)

SCAN

Tweeting with GOD will help your group to

- think about the faith and see the logic of God's plan for mankind
- grow in their relationship with Jesus
- pray and share the faith together
- put their faith into action

#TwGOD sessions

- start with questions of the group members themselves
- are accessible to everyone
- encourage participants to think for themselves
- give suggestions for living the faith on a daily basis
- take place in an atmosphere of trust and friendship
- allow room for holding and expressing different opinions
- start and finish with a moment of prayer, putting everything in God's hands

Make a plan

Now it is time to make your ideas concrete. How often are you going to meet, and what is the schedule for the season? (SEE APPENDIX 1). The atmosphere of the meetings is important: Where and in what setting are you going to meet? (SEE B.4). How are you going to invite people? (SEE APPENDIX 1). How will you collect the questions (SEE B.3), and do you intend to have a special first session? (SEE APPENDIX 1). An adult group will be more likely to dive right into the questions, whereas a group of teens might need more ice-breaking activities.

> Get some people together to form a team, know your objectives and vision, and start to Tweet with God!

B.2 What does a typical session look like?

S tart by deciding which questions you will discuss during this session (see B.3). It is a good idea for the group to prepare themselves by reading some material on the topic beforehand. See our suggestions for using #TwGOD with a group (see A.5) and our description of the format of the original #TwGOD sessions (see A.1). If this is the first of a series of sessions, it is important to think about a proper order for discussing the questions, taking into account both the questions from the group and the liturgical seasons of the Church (see Appendix 1).

Starting the session

Start the session with a brief opening prayer, led, if possible, by one of the group members (see Appendix 5). When new people are present, introductions are a good idea; for example, ask everyone to tell his name and the color of his socks (see Appendix 3). Agree with everyone on the #TwGOD rules that will help the discussion to take place in a positive and peaceful environment (see A.2). Whatever the topic, there are always reasons to have a good laugh and have fun together. This is a natural way to release tension and to bring the group together.

Discussing the topic

Next it is time to present the question at hand; for example: "Doesn't the Big Bang rule out faith in God?" (see Tweet 1.1). There are several ways to help the group discuss the topic (see Appendices 2 and 3).

- The person who posed the question may explain why he chose it and give his preliminary ideas about it.
- Another way to start the discussion is to ask a group member to prepare beforehand a brief presentation on the content of the answer in the #TwGOD book.

Subsequently, others in the group can say that they agree and for what reason, or present their own opinions and argumentation. If they do not have an opinion ready, you can ask a subquestion (see B.5); for

Suggested timetable in minutes

Depending on your group, you can discuss two or more questions (Tweets) during a session. This schedule allows for discussion of two questions. You can alter it as you wish.

00.00	Opening prayer by a group member
00.02	Presentation of new people; agree on #TwGOD rules
00.05	*Input:* introduction to the first Tweet by a group member
00.10	*Discussion round 1*
00.40	*Input:* read more material (using the app to move online from the book)
00.45	*Discussion round 2*
01.05	*Summary:* by the group leader or by reading the book together
01.10	*Input:* introduction to the second Tweet
01.15	*Discussion round 1*
01.45	*Input:* read more material
01.50	*Discussion round 2*
02.10	*Summary*
02.15	Closing prayer in a church or chapel
02.30	End

SCAN

example: "How can you reconcile the story of Creation in Genesis with the theory of evolution?" "Did you ever think about this?" "Is the Church against space travel?" "Can science ever find proof of the existence of God?" "Is that important for your faith?"

After everyone has had a chance to contribute to the discussion, it may be helpful to use the #TwGOD app to access the "Read more" material. This way, you can read related quotes from the *Catechism of the Catholic Church* (and its *Compendium*) and the *Youth Catechism of the Catholic Church* (YOUCAT). You will also find quotes from various popes and Fathers of the Church. That should help to start a second round of discussion.

Rounding off

To round off the discussion, you can give a summary of what has been said, if you feel up to it, or read the text of the book together, recognizing which arguments were mentioned by the group. An important question at this point is: "How does this relate to my personal faith and relationship with Jesus?" This can be mentioned in the summary. Next, ask yourselves how you can make what you have learned part of your life. These questions can lead into the prayer at the end. Conclude the session, preferably in the church or a chapel, with a liturgical form of prayer, such as Compline or a moment of adoration (SEE APPENDIX 5).

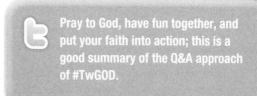

Pray to God, have fun together, and put your faith into action; this is a good summary of the Q&A approach of #TwGOD.

23

B.3 Which questions shall we discuss?

Ideally the group itself should decide which questions to discuss during the *Tweeting with GOD* sessions. You can prepare the first session together by taking a survey of all the questions the people in your group would like to address. It is easiest to ask the group members to submit their questions in writing: on paper, through e-mail, or through social media. The full list will contain all kinds of questions, and organizing them will require some work.

#Trim the list

Decide as a group leader or together with the team which questions are too private or otherwise unsuitable to be discussed in the group. These may be discussed privately, or you can refer the askers to someone who can help them answer those questions.

Group and plan

You will find that certain questions relate to the same topic. Put them together in groups. It is our experience that the order presented in the book is a useful one, as it starts with the basics of the faith that are needed to understand other issues. For example, if you want to use the Bible as a reliable guide, you will first have to discuss the reasons the Church considers the Bible trustworthy (SEE TWEETS 1.10–1.21).

So, you could start with the first question posed by your group that occurs in the book. In a later stage, the order is less important, and you can speak during one session about Christian ethics (SEE TWEETS 4.1–4.50) and during the next about the history of the Church (SEE TWEETS 2.1–2.50), for example. Occasionally, a question may not be covered in the book. When this occurs, please let us know through social media. Also, you can address such questions using the same method described above.

Once you have ordered the questions, determine which topics you are going to discuss during each session. You may wish to create a calendar, so that the participants can prepare themselves for the sessions.

Bonding and building trust

For the #TwGOD sessions to be fruitful, it is important to create an atmosphere of bonding and trust within the group.

- Agree with all participants on the #TwGOD rules (SEE A.2 AND B.1).
- Avoid inviting people for one session only, as this may erode the atmosphere of trust.
- Invest time and effort in helping the participants to get to know each other (SEE APPENDIX 3 FOR FUN WAYS).

The greater the trust, the greater the ease group members will feel with each other, which will make not only deeper discussions possible but also deeper relationships. Friendships between participants will help them to continue the #TwGOD sessions, despite their busy schedules!

Eliciting questions

Sometimes the survey needs the help of an interactive method (SEE APPENDICES 2 AND 3). The participants may be too shy or otherwise unwilling to send in questions beforehand. If this is the case, you may wish to use the first session to take stock of the group's questions. You will see that one question will lead to another.

....

Moderating the discussion

The group leader acts as a moderator. Especially if your group has some experience together and a certain level of trust, time will be up before you know it. Do not be afraid of some silence: people need time to think before they speak. However, longer periods of silence in a group can be very awkward. You can ask some questions to keep the discussion going (SEE B.5 AND APPENDIX 2). You will find that many subtopics will come up during the discussions. In discussing Tweet 1.1, for example, people might ask about the link between man and ape, the size of the universe, and the existence of aliens. Adam and Eve will probably come up. It is important not to let the discussion become too broad. If a question is off the topic, you can decide to discuss it during the next session.

Spending time with each other in a comfortable environment builds an atmosphere of trust among those present (SEE Box); by seeing the others face-to-face, participants may feel comfortable enough to pose their own questions. Therefore, be sure to create a safe, welcoming setting (SEE B.4).

> Questions come from the participants: #TwGOD always starts with their questions. One question will lead to another.

B.4 Where and in what setting can we hold our #TwGOD sessions?

Tweeting with GOD sessions can be held anywhere the participants feel welcome. Some people find it quite difficult to speak about God. A hospitable setting can contribute a lot to making them feel comfortable. This begins with an atmosphere of trust within the group (SEE B.3); the brief #TwGOD rules can help with this (SEE B.1).

Choosing a place and time
When you are deciding on a location and time for your #TwGOD sessions, it is good to check with the potential participants about their expectations and availability. As a general rule, the following considerations may be useful.

Participants' interest
Place yourself in the shoes of the participants and consider what makes them happy. You don't need much, but creating a particular setting may help to promote that atmosphere of trust you are looking for (SEE B.3). Teens love chips and soda, college students enjoy having a drink together, and adults might prefer a cup of coffee or tea, or maybe dinner. You may wish to be careful with alcohol. When you are deciding on the setting, our suggestions may be of help (SEE Box).

Participants' schedules
The time depends mostly on the availability of the participants.
- When your focus is on teenagers, keep in mind that they may be occupied with sports or other activities on Saturdays and have homework on weeknights.
- If you have young parents in your group, they will wish to eat dinner with their family and might prefer to meet after dinnertime.
- College students have exams that need to be taken into account.

Make that dusty, boring parish hall look cozy!

The only available location may be that drab, dusty old room in your parish center. How can you ever make your group feel welcome there? We would apply a few simple tricks: collect some tablecloths, candles, and plants (artificial plants last almost forever). In a thrift shop you might even find some appealing tableware and something like a folding screen, on which you can hang some posters or pictures. You could do this by yourself, although getting the group involved can help to build camaraderie. We assure you: you will be surprised at the result!

Suggestion 1: In the pub

Where:	In a pub (or a parish hall decorated comfortably)
When:	On a weekend night
Target group:	College students
Supplies:	Drinks, snacks
Atmosphere:	Cushions, candles, and so forth
Tip:	Make sure you select a location that is not too crowded: you want to be able to hear each other.

Suggestion 2: Over dinner

Where:	In your parish center or in someone's home
When:	Any evening
Target group:	Students or other adults
Supplies:	Ingredients and a kitchen
Atmosphere:	A nice tablecloth, candles, dimmed light
Tip:	If possible, cook together. This allows for low-key contact between participants and gives you insight into the group dynamics.

Suggestion 3: With coffee or brunch

Where:	In your parish center or in someone's home
When:	After morning Mass on Sundays
Target group:	Any group
Supplies:	Coffee, tea, muffins, cake, sandwiches
Atmosphere:	A nice tablecloth and napkins
Tip:	Make it a potluck brunch, where everyone brings some food.

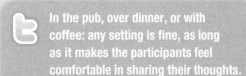

In the pub, over dinner, or with coffee: any setting is fine, as long as it makes the participants feel comfortable in sharing their thoughts.

27

B.5 Do you have any practical advice for the group leader?

Whether or not you have had experience as a group leader in moderating discussions, it is important to keep striving to become a better leader and a better Christian. On these pages we list what we consider the most important dos and don'ts for moderating #TwGOD sessions, although this list is not exhaustive. We hope this will help you to recognize that it does not take very much to be a good group leader. By following these few tips, you will be well on your way to becoming the best group leader you can be! That way, the sessions will be inspiring for you too.

Dos

1. *Pray!* Ask God to guide you in your preparation and during the #TwGOD sessions. Remember that you do not have to do this alone!

2. *Walk the talk.* Be aware that you function as a role model to your group. Teens in particular are highly impressionable: if you lead their *Tweeting with GOD* session on Friday night, and they see you drunk on Saturday night, you lose credibility.

3. *Prepare well.* Sometimes you can't help having things go wrong, but do your best to make the meetings go smoothly. This includes preparing the questions (and possible answers) and all materials you will need.

4. *Do it together.* Involve the participants in the planning, for starters with the selecting and grouping of questions (SEE B.3), and also with the inviting, shopping, etc. You may struggle with delegating, and it may take more time than doing things yourself; but your job is to build up the group.

5. *Encourage and thank.* A word of encouragement or thanks goes a long way. Teens especially may feel insecure and self-conscious and need positive feedback. Compliment those who cooked, thank those who cleaned up, and comfort those who became emotional.

Don'ts

1. *Don't speak all the time.* Sure, you can share your own experiences if doing so is conducive to the conversation, but try to give the floor to the participants and their personal stories and questions.

2. *Don't just share information; share a vision.* Mere information just doesn't appeal. The beauty of our faith is that it involves us in a dynamic relationship with the God who loves us!

3. *Don't put people on the spot*, especially not in the beginning. Not everyone is comfortable praying in public or speaking about his personal opinion. You can always ask for a volunteer. When the group gets to know each other better, you can sometimes gently encourage shy members to speak.

4. *Don't use Church jargon* without an explanation. Words such as *Eucharist*, *grace,* and *sin* are not familiar to all people. #TwGOD is about getting to know the faith, not about feeling excluded if you do not know everything yet.

5. *Don't be discouraged if your group is small.* It's quality not quantity that counts. Your #TwGOD group is a safe place for people to discover the faith step by step, not a factory producing first-class theologians by the dozens.

Breaking down the questions

Depending on the background of the participants, a question such as "Was Jesus against women?" (SEE TWEET 2.16) might need to be broken down to be discussed fruitfully in the group (SEE B.2). A good starting question is "Why do you ask?" Some of the subquestions will come to you when you read the text of the Tweet during your preparation. In the case of Tweet 2.16, for example, you'll want the participants to think of what they know of Jesus: Did he treat men and women differently? Were there women Apostles? Why not? Are man and woman the same in every respect? What does the Bible say? Do the differences between the sexes matter?

Be yourself

The most important rule for dealing with a group, and especially a group of young people, is to be authentic: be yourself! Be willing to share your personal faith and convictions. Be open even about what you do not know (yet). Be careful, however, not to discourage the group in their search for the answers to their questions. Your doubts about certain issues may not be suitable for sharing here; keep them for when you meet your spiritual director (SEE TWEETS 3.4 AND 4.6). Try to be positive at all times!

 It mainly takes dedication and conviction to be a good group leader; be yourself and do not be afraid of not having all the answers.

29

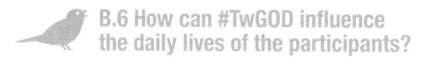

B.6 How can #TwGOD influence the daily lives of the participants?

The message of Jesus, the gospel, is not meant to be only talked about; it is meant to be lived! During the *Tweeting with GOD* sessions, participants learn not only about God and his unending love but also about his Church and his plan for the world. Thus, there is a link between knowing God and serving him in our daily lives. For this connection to be experienced by the members of your group, it helps to pray together and to do works of mercy together. But don't forget to do fun activities too, for the Christian life is full of joy.

In addition to learning about the faith, #TwGOD groups have three other elements: they pray, have fun, and act charitably.

Pray

Prayer is essential if you wish to grow in knowledge of God, as faith is in the first place about a relationship. Hence the importance of starting and concluding the sessions with prayer.

There are other ways the group can pray together. You could, for example, attend Mass together or spend time in adoration before the Blessed Sacrament. The participants can be involved by expressing their prayer intentions, singing, and playing music (SEE APPENDICES 1, 5, AND 6).

Have fun

It is not Catholic to have serious faces all the time. God is not like that! If we believe that he loves us, that he saves us, then we can be lighthearted at times. Humor can help a lot in making a profound and serious discussion more interesting. So, every #TwGOD session should have an element of fun.

Often, it can be very important for the group to do something else together, apart from the #TwGOD sessions about questions related to the faith. Don't be afraid to go out and have some good fun together! You could go sailing or hiking, have a picnic or

---

Jesus, prayer, and witness

Jesus: "If we forge ahead with our own arrangements, with other things, with beautiful things but without Jesus we make no headway, it does not work. Jesus is more important."

Prayer: "Looking at the face of God, but above all … realizing that he is also looking at us. The Lord looks at us. He looks at us first."

Witness: "Faith can only be communicated through witness, and that means love. Not with our own ideas but with the Gospel, lived out in our own lives and brought to life within us by the Holy Spirit."

(POPE FRANCIS TO NEW MOVEMENTS, MAY 18, 2013)

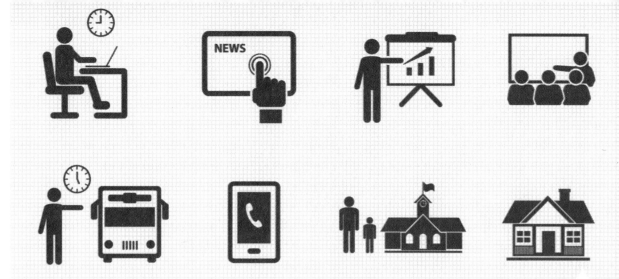

a barbecue, watch a movie or play board games, anything. The goal is to get to know each other better, make some new friends, and enjoy spending time together. Being a Catholic is not boring! You will see that by doing fun activities together, your discussion sessions will become more lively.

#Act charitably

The Catholic faith does not consist only of intellectual knowledge. Hopefully, the knowledge gathered by participants during the #TwGOD sessions will lead them to grow in their personal relationship with Jesus. This friendship with God will in turn stimulate concern for others and the desire to act charitably toward those in need.

It is good to make plans together for a charitable activity with the #TwGOD group. Discuss together where you would like to help out; for example, in a nursing home, at a food bank, or with an after-school program for underprivileged children. Every participant can contribute in his own way. You may wish to dedicate some time to talking about how the participants experienced the activity. You will find that their hearts and perspectives on the world will be changed through doing generous acts.

> Think, pray, and act in a positive and joyful way. These are the main ingredients of every #TwGOD activity.

Part C
Multiple uses of #TwGOD

Introduction

*T*weeting with GOD has proven to be useful for virtually everyone who desires to learn something about the Catholic faith, especially because it helps people to think for themselves about how logical our faith is. The tools of #TwGOD (see C.1) are designed in such a way that they can be used by participants with different needs and expectations, either alone or in a group. The overall aim is to demonstrate the beauty of our Catholic faith and to help people to become more involved in their relationship with God and in explaining their faith to others.

The program is intended for everyone above the age of 12 or 13, who is starting to think about the faith and is looking for answers but does not necessarily have a lot of background knowledge. That includes those who wish to become Catholic and those who are preparing to receive the Sacraments of Baptism, Confirmation, Eucharist, or Marriage. It also includes parents and all those related to children who are beginning to ask difficult questions about the faith.

Thus the #TwGOD program is for those who want to
- think about what they believe and why they believe it
- learn more about the Catholic faith and grow in their relationship with Jesus
- share their faith with others and be able to answer (difficult) questions about it
- give their faith as a present to others by giving away the #TwGOD book

In this third part of the #TwGOD manual, we first want to share with you some more information about the #TwGOD project in its entirety. Then we will focus on specific groups of users and how they can find the answers to their questions through the program.

Our intention is always to help people on their path to God by encouraging them to discuss the content of the faith. In the words of Jesus: "The good man out of the good treasure of the heart produces good ... for out of the abundance of the heart the mouth speaks" (Lk. 6:45); therefore you cannot be quiet about that which you profoundly love. Ultimately, *Tweeting with GOD* is about love indeed, the great love that God has for every single person.

Tweeting with God means engaging in a loving relationship and a dialogue with him, while searching to live accordingly. We hope that *Tweeting with GOD* may help many people to discover the love of God for them and to formulate an answer to that love. He is waiting patiently!

Tweeting with GOD is based on five tools, created and managed, in part, by young people and a priest: a book, a website, an app, social media, and videos. These tools are closely interconnected.

Book

The book can be used either alone as a source of study and reference regarding the faith or as a means to foster dialogue in groups (SEE B.1–B.6). The 200 questions and answers are divided into four sections, which are preceded by an encouraging introduction by a bishop. Of all the #TwGOD tools, the book gives the most extensive answers to the questions. It is not necessary to read the book from cover to cover. You can go directly to the question that interests you. The references within parentheses direct you to related questions in the book. It is our hope that you will enjoy many hours of reading or browsing through the book, just as you might do online.

#Website and app

Speaking of online: the "Read more" section at the bottom of each right-hand page in the book is directly related to the "From the wisdom of the Church" section on the particular web page dedicated to that Tweet. The "Read more" section points the reader toward relevant information in the YOUCAT, the *Catechism of the Catholic Church*, and its *Compendium*. The particular page can be found by browsing the website tweetingwithgod.com or by using the smartphone application. The web page also shows other related texts from various popes and Fathers of the Church. The "Read more" section is therefore a wonderful tool for further study.

An easier way to access the extra reading material online is by using the app. With its scan technology, the app links the printed text to online content (SEE B.1). By scanning the photo of a Tweet in the book, indicated with the SCAN logo, you will end up directly on the corresponding

Are new questions added to #TwGOD?

Just as at the origin of #TwGOD (SEE A.1), we still receive questions related to the faith through all kinds of media: Twitter, Facebook, e-mail, on paper, you name it! The team members collect these questions and formulate short, cohesive answers, which are written together with a priest and are then posted on Facebook. If, for any reason, an answer is not suitable for public posting, we send it to the asker directly.

Multiple uses of #TwGOD

SCAN

web page, embedded in the app. The application also contains the texts for Mass and dozens of prayers, available in languages ranging from Portuguese to Russian and from Latin to Polish. These make the app like a portable liturgy and prayer book, ideal for travel! Also, many priests have told us how the app has helped them when concelebrating Mass or hearing confessions in a different language. The app is very useful to access the "Read more" material with your group (SEE B.2).

Social media and video

The young people behind #TwGOD run several social media accounts, where they connect with their peers. These provide inspirational quotes, encouraging videos, funny quizzes, and insightful behind-the-scenes information. The team members also welcome questions and answer them with the help of Fr. Michel. After all, questions are at the heart of the #TwGOD project!

In order to make #TwGOD come alive, we publish videos created by people from various countries. These videos range from Christmas greetings to explanations of different aspects of the faith.

> The multimedia project #TwGOD is based on five closely interconnected pillars: a book, a website, an app, social media, and videos.

Multiple uses of #TwGOD

Depending on the age of your group, you could use #TwGOD in different ways in a Confirmation class. Young people age 13 and older can read the book for themselves (SEE B.1–B.6). The book might be too difficult for those younger than 13. If you have younger children in your group, you can still follow the suggestions below. Just read the corresponding sections from the book yourself and then present the information to the group in your own words. The book also is a great reference for answering difficult questions!

Curriculum

Confirmation programs vary from diocese to diocese. While we are confident that everything someone needs to know for Confirmation is in #TwGOD, we suggest you check with your diocesan guidelines in order to know which questions need to be covered as a minimum. Even so, questions from the group should still be given a very imporant place. When you talk to young people about topics of interest to them, they pay attention and remember what you say. This manual includes suggested topics for Confirmation classes (SEE APPENDIX 6). Of course, you can let the topics partly depend on the questions presented by the group. The younger the group, the more the group leader will need to do, both as a moderater and in answering questions.

Play and learn

Especially when the group is quite young, it is not possible to use the entire session for discussion. You will need to introduce some playful elements and maybe some sports too. We offer you a few ideas (SEE BOX AND APPENDICES 2 AND 3), and you can invent your own. It is great when the activity or the game

Dialogue with a priest

Fr. Michel: In the parish, it was one of my tasks to help with preparing the children for Confirmation, together with a small team of volunteers. That was great fun! The children were usually 11 or 12 years old, and we would use an existing course, which we adapted where necessary. The sessions I remember best were those when we addressed the questions of the children. They too would often say that they enjoyed these sessions. What struck me most was the remark of a little girl: "I have never had a chance to speak to a priest before."

Of course, the questions sometimes went completely off topic, but isn't it better to speak about something interesting to children whose eyes are shining enthusiastically than to speak about something they consider boring? We would make sure that by the end of the preparation course we had covered all of the material the children needed to know. I know this can be difficult at times, but wouldn't it be great for every child preparing for Confirmation to have at least two sessions of dialogue with a priest?

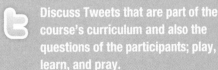

helps to deepen the understanding of the topic. For this reason, it is a good idea to give some homework: reading a Tweet, learning a prayer by heart, making a report or a drawing, and so forth. Because the impact of the topic on the life of the participants is of great importance, it is good to integrate this into the discussion, or at least into the conclusion. If no priest is involved in the team, invite your priest at least once to engage in dialogue with the participants (SEE BOX).

Pray together

The concluding prayer time is essential to demonstrate that the Catholic faith is all about a personal relationship with God. It is also an introduction to different forms of prayer (praise, adoration, intercessions, the Rosary, lighting candles, and so forth). Variation is good. Regularly pray important prayers such as the Our Father, the Hail Mary, and the Apostles' Creed, inviting all to learn these by heart.

Structure of a Confirmation class

- Brief opening prayer (if possible, led by a participant)
- Review of the last session and the homework
- Presentation of the topic (possibly by a participant)
- Questions and group discussion
- Snack break
- Play an appropriate game or stage a playful presentation that reinforces the topic
- Group discussion about how the lesson relates to everyday life
- Closing prayer (if possible, in the church or a chapel)

> Discuss Tweets that are part of the course's curriculum and also the questions of the participants; play, learn, and pray.

C.3 Can #TwGOD replace our marriage preparation or RCIA classes?

First of all, with *Tweeting with GOD* we do not intend to replace anything. In many places, there are very good initiatives in the various fields of catechesis, and in particular for those preparing to receive one of the sacraments, be it Baptism, Confirmation, first holy Communion, or Marriage. In other places, organized preparation is unfortunately lacking. If #TwGOD can play a role in people's catechetical formation, helping them to learn about the faith in relation to their personal path through life with God, that is great.

At the very least, #TwGOD has proven to be a good reference work to be used by those involved in different forms of catechesis. They can use the book and the online material to explore a topic presented in a catechetical class or to find answers to the many questions that arise in studying catechetical materials.

Preparing for marriage

#TwGOD often speaks of marriage, as this is an essential institution (SEE TWEETS 4.43 AND 4.19–4.21); hence the importance of a good preparation. Usually a priest will guide you in your preparation for the great day. In addition, you can read the Tweets related to marriage, always with an eye for the greater picture of the faith, which is God's love for us (SEE TWEET 1.27). It would be helpful to read also the other parts of the book, so as to situate your marriage within the plan of God for mankind.

Furthermore, you could read three Bible texts and speak with your future spouse about these. The first is about the marriage at Cana (JN. 2:1–12): is it without meaning that Jesus starts his public life at a marriage? The second is about the way spouses should live together in total surrender to each other (EPH. 5:21–33): ladies, don't get angry about your submissive role before you read the fate of men: they must be humbled, suffer, and die for you as Christ did for the Church. The third is about the duration of marriage (MT. 19:1–12): it is a bond for all your life.

> ### "I learned about Catholicism"
>
> Ashley: The #TwGOD sessions helped me to discover the Catholic faith gradually when I was not yet a Catholic. There were so many things I did not know about the Catholic Church. Through weekly meetings with other young people, my questions about the faith were answered. Thus I learned a lot about Catholicism and my own faith.
>
> Many people have questions about the faith, and I find it important for these questions to be answered honestly. Fortunately this is now possible for everyone because of the #TwGOD project.

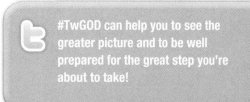

God's answers in the Bible

When you are preparing to become a Catholic and to receive the sacraments, the most important thing is prayer. The Bible can help you to pray, but as you read it, you will come across many things you do not understand (SEE TWEETS 1.10–1.25). Then you will need someone to help you, as did the court official who was reading from the prophet Isaiah in his chariot. When he met the Apostle Philip, who asked him whether he understood what he was reading, the official replied: "How can I, unless some one guides me?" (ACTS 8:31). Thanks to the guidance of Philip, this official decided to be baptized.

We all need help and guidance on our path with Jesus. The role of a spiritual director, like the Apostle Philip, is very important (SEE TWEETS 3.4 AND 4.6). If you are thinking about being baptized or about becoming a Catholic, have a chat with a priest.

Knowledge about the faith

Even if only to explain to your friends why you are marrying in the Church or becoming a Catholic, you will need some factual information about the faith. This will also help you in your relationship with Jesus, which is what faith is all about. Knowledge about the faith will help you to make important decisions with both your heart and your mind.

> #TwGOD can help you to see the greater picture and to be well prepared for the great step you're about to take!

C.4 How can #TwGOD help parents and godparents?

Do you fear the questions of your child, godchild, or grandchild about the faith? Do you dread the moment your child returns from a sacrament preparation class? Some parishes are great at involving the parents in their child's preparation for first holy Communion and Confirmation. In some places, however, the role of the parents is limited to bringing their child to and from class.

Answering questions

This is where #TwGOD can help you! First of all, the program can serve as a reference for answering all kinds of questions about the faith, whatever the occasion. By using the book's index, the website, or the app, you will be able to find the answers to your child's questions. You will soon be very skilled in finding the answers quickly! And you may learn something yourself on the way!

Furthermore, as you are using #TwGOD to find answers to particular questions, you will discover many other interesting topics. #TwGOD is designed so that you can browse from one topic to another, led by your curiosity. Before you know it, you'll have read the answer to a question before your child even asks it.

"I grew in my relationship with God"

Lodewijk: In the weekly #TwGOD sessions, I learned a lot about the faith and about bringing it into practice in my daily life. They gave me a good combination of knowledge about the faith and practical tips on how to be a Christian in everyday life. Because we studied all the main topics of the faith and discussed them under the guidance of Fr. Michel, I learned how to explain the faith to others and to understand it myself.

#TwGOD has strengthened my relationship with God and has made me realize that being a Christian means more than going to Church once a week: it is truly a personal relationship with God. I am very grateful for the knowledge I gained in such a short time. It has given me a lot of material for my personal journey with God. I hope to be able to share all this later with my children!

SCAN

#Work ahead!

In conjunction with your child's sacramental preparation, you can read the topics in #TwGOD that are covered in his course. Thus you will be well prepared to engage in a dialogue about the faith with your child. This works even better if it is done by a group of parents or godparents who get together to follow a curriculum using #TwGOD that is similar to their children's course. Apart from getting ready to answer difficult questions, this is a chance to grow in your personal faith with others seeking to do the same thing (SEE B.1–B.6).

Every parish or diocese has its own curriculum for preparing children to receive sacraments. If you compare the table of contents in your diocese's curriculum with the #TwGOD index, or use the app or the online search tool, you will quickly find which Tweets to read.

Dare not to know

As we said to group leaders, there is no need to be afraid of not knowing an answer (SEE B.5). No one can know everything! Not knowing may be a great start for a joint adventure in searching for the answer together with your child and perhaps his godparents and grand-parents. You may end up asking certain ques-tions of your priest. These are all occasions to share the faith.

> #TwGOD can serve as both a powerful reference and a way to prepare yourself for questions you can expect.

C.5 What role can #TwGOD play in ecumenism and interreligious dialogue?

Ecumenism is the common search for unity between separated Christians (SEE TWEET 2.12). This separation is most unfortunate and a scandal; we are all called to cooperate with the Holy Spirit in the search for renewed unity.

In search of the Truth

Care should be taken, however, to lose nothing of the truth about God. If we truly believe there is only one Truth (SEE TWEET 1.8), real ecumenism means that we cherish what we have received as Truth in the Tradition of our Church. Thus, ecumenism does not mean that we simply pick what we like from the different Christian traditions, as that would imply that belief is merely a matter of taste. #TwGOD is written from a clearly Catholic point of view, true to the traditions and the teachings of the Catholic Church. At the same time, we have tried to speak about other traditions in a respectful way.

Catholics and all Christians

We are convinced that whoever wishes to be involved in serious ecumenical dialogue needs a solid knowledge about the faith of his own church before he can speak about it with others. This knowledge must be based not only on external, theoretical knowledge but also on personal faith in the love of God and his presence in our lives.

As Catholics, we are called continually to learn more about our faith, which is the basis of our relationship with Jesus Christ. The #TwGOD project can help Catholics to deepen their faith on both an intellectual and personal level. With this knowledge and experience of our faith as a basis, we can then start studying the beliefs of our fellow Christians in the search for unity.

St. John Paul II on ecumenism and truth

Ecumenism implies that the Christian communities should help one another so that there may be truly present in them the full content and all the requirements of "the heritage handed down by the Apostles". Without this, full communion will never be possible.... In this courageous journey towards unity, the transparency and the prudence of faith require us to avoid both false irenicism and indifference to the Church's ordinances. Conversely, that same transparency and prudence urge us to reject a halfhearted commitment to unity....

To uphold a vision of unity which takes account of all the demands of revealed truth does not mean to put a brake on the ecumenical movement. On the contrary, it means preventing it from settling for apparent solutions which would lead to no firm and solid results. The obligation to respect the Truth is absolute. Is this not the law of the Gospel? (JOHN PAUL II, ENCYCLICAL LETTER *Ut unum sint*, MAY 25, 1995, 78–79)

SCAN

The same applies for Christians of other denominations: after they have studied and experienced their own beliefs, the #TwGOD program may help them to grasp the essence of the Catholic view. Such a mutual understanding of what is important to each of us is essential for a dialogue that is both true to our own faith and open to the views of others (SEE A.2).

Interreligious dialogue?

People often confuse ecumenism with interreligious dialogue. These are not the same, however. Dialogue between a Catholic and a Protestant or an Orthodox is based on a common belief in salvation by Jesus Christ, which is essential to us all. That common factor is lacking in interreligious dialogue, which therefore is not aimed at working toward full unity in Christ.

Rather, with representatives of other religions, the dialogue will remain mostly at the level of mutual respect and of the desire to cooperate on concrete charitable or political projects. Still, for a proper dialogue to take place, knowledge of your own faith and at least a general idea of the beliefs of the other person are essential. Again, #TwGOD can be a useful instrument to provide this basic knowledge.

> Only when you know what you believe can you engage in dialogue with others, respecting what is different, sharing what you have in common.

C.6 How does #TwGOD contribute to the New Evangelization?

We live in a time of both great possibilities and challenges. Today it almost seems as if man is able to do and to make anything, provided he has the financial means. Many great developments have been accomplished. At the same time, it is important to remain connected with the source of our humanity and to see the greater picture (SEE TWEET 1.27). Thinking about this leads to many questions.

By providing answers to even the most daring questions regarding the faith, with #TwGOD we hope to contribute to a generation of faithful who are credible, confident witnesses of Christ's message—not primarily because they know so much about the faith, but because they have a personal relationship with Jesus, who calls them to act. We are conscious that we need to use every means, including all suitable modern media, to spread his message of love. All recent popes have called for a renewed explanation of the faith, for a New Evangelization (SEE TWEET 4.50).

Everyday life

Although they may have heard of Jesus Christ, many people do not see how he could possibly be relevant to their everyday lives. #TwGOD goes out to meet them in those places where they spend a lot of their time: on their computers and phones. Through the different #TwGOD tools (SEE C1), faith becomes an integral part of the media they use.

> **"My relationship with God became stronger"**
>
> Gerard: Everyone reaches this point in their faith where they start wondering whether what the Bible teaches is true or not. You begin to ask questions, and often you don't come to an answer on your own.
>
> I was lucky that during that point in my faith journey #TwGOD was founded. Within this group a number of my peers and I discussed our questions under the guidance of Fr. Michel. By thinking about these questions together, we found answers that we would have never found on our own. Moreover, questions were posed that I myself hadn't really thought about yet.
>
> After several #TwGOD sessions I had the feeling that my relationship with God was being strengthened and that praying to him became easier. Now, in my daily life, I am better able to explain to people why God is important to me, whereas previously I would sometimes have difficulty doing that.

Into the world

Learning about the faith is important, but faith cannot be limited to intellectual knowledge. On the contrary! We cannot speak about faith, hope, and love without putting them into practice. Every Christian is called to go out into the world and to love our neighbor as Jesus loves us. Scripture tells us how he is particularly present in the most needy in our society: the poor, the homeless, the disabled, the elderly, the unhappy (Mt. 25:31–46). As we learn to share ourselves with them, let us also share what is dearest to us, our faith. Therefore, Pope St. John Paul II (see Tweet 2.50) was a fervent advocate of ever renewed efforts to evangelize. He said: "It is more necessary than ever for all the faithful to move from a faith of habit, sustained perhaps by social context alone, to a faith which is conscious and personally lived. The renewal of faith will always be the best way to lead others to the Truth that is Christ" (John Paul II, Ecclesia in America, Jan. 22, 1999).

Tweet with God!

The #TwGOD tools are intended to inform, to encourage, and to entertain. Yet #TwGOD is not a magic formula: ultimately our hearts can be converted only by God. It is he who speaks to each of us and inspires us to go out and meet our brothers and sisters, to follow his Will for our lives, to seek and to give forgiveness, and to do so much more. We pray that #TwGOD may help many people to draw nearer to God.

> By helping people to realize what is most important in life and to find answers to their questions, #TwGOD helps them to proclaim the gospel.

Appendix 1: A season with #TwGOD

Here is an example of what a season of #TwGOD sessions may look like. Feel free to adapt it to your own needs. The sessions should always be based on the questions of the participants (SEE A.2). Involve them as much as possible in the preparations and in the team. For more ideas and for free downloads see www.tweetingwithgod.com/howto.

Preliminary preparations (SEE B.1)
- Form a team with a group leader.
- Share your vision (the reason for doing this).
- Make a plan (target group, time, and location).
- Make a calendar, taking into account the celebrations of the liturgical year (Advent, Christmas, Lent, Easter, Pentecost).

Team: Invitations & publicity

Week 1: Kickoff party
- Begin with an enjoyable event: barbecue, picnic, party, etc.
- Have everyone say his name and something about himself.
- Have a fun warm-up activity.
- Introduce #TwGOD: concept, materials, calendar, etc.

Week 2: First meeting
- Spend time getting to know each other better.
- Collect questions (SEE APPENDIX 3).

Team: Organizing questions & planning (SEE B.3)

Week 3: #TwGOD Meeting 1 (SEE B.2)

Week 4: #TwGOD Meeting 2 (SEE B.2)

Team: Evaluation & team building

Week 5: #TwGOD Meeting 3

Weekend in week 5: Pray
- Have a prayer session together.

Week 6: #TwGOD Meeting 4

Week 7: #TwGOD Meeting 5

Weekend in week 7: Have fun
- Do something together.

Week 8: #TwGOD Meeting 6

Team: Evaluation & team building

Week 9: #TwGOD Meeting 7

Weekend in week 9: Act
- Work together to help others.

Week 10: #TwGOD Meeting 8

Week 11: #TwGOD Meeting 9

Continue until final week

Team: Evaluation

Weekend in last week: Closing party

Appendix 2: Encouraging participants to ask questions

Especially when working with teenagers, it can be quite a challenge to get your group to talk. They may not be used to thinking for themselves and expressing their opinions. But it is vital that you encourage them to speak because our faith is based not only on what others tell us but on a conscious choice for God. And such a choice can be made only when we are well informed about the faith. On a more practical note, when you manage to get the conversation going, the teens will show that they can indeed engage in dialogue and actually enjoy doing so! The following points will also work for older groups that have difficulty in starting.

Why is it so difficult?

How often is a teenager seriously asked for his opinion, and how often is the one asking for it really interested? Teens simply are not (yet) used to being listened to! A teenager – even more than an adult – looks at the world from his own perspective. Life often seems to be a fight. As a result, the world is about himself in the first place, and only then about himself in relation to others. Paradoxically, teens are very concerned about others' opinions of them. Of course, there are many other elements to keep in mind, but the ones mentioned here can be of help in stimulating the conversation.

To speak in front of a group of people can be challenging, especially if you do not know them. See Appendix 3 for some fun methods to break the ice and to start smiling at each other. As in all groups, getting to the first question is the most challenging, as usually one question generates other questions. But do not be too quick to ask the first question yourself. An awkward silence can be helpful in getting people to think (SEE B.3 AND B.5).

From question to questions

Asking the group some direct questions may help them to begin a conversation. A great way to get them involved is by asking, "Who has a question about the faith?" If you are lucky, a few people will raise their hands and you can begin

with their questions. However, to get everyone involved you can first ask the following question: "Who does *not* have any questions about God or the faith?" Now all those who did not respond to the first question should raise their hands, but they will realize that they have not answered truthfully. There you are: you just got your group to start thinking!

Different differences

You can also ask the group about a time when someone questioned them about their faith. Or: "Which of you sometimes talks about the faith with friends? What do you speak about?" People often experience a clash between their daily lives in society and their faith. Where does this clash occur? Do those in the group consider themselves to be different from other people in society? If a teen says: "My friends do not believe, and I do," you can ask: "How do you deal with that difference?"

To be more provocative, you can ask the group: "Do you believe everything the Church teaches?" If they are honest, there will be some reactions here. Usually the answer will be no. Do not be afraid of provocative or almost aggressive answers (SEE A.2): your task is to stimulate a line of thought, not to indoctrinate the group with your own view. If your view is good, they will come to see its logic eventually. But it will be worth much more if they themselves come to find the answer.

Appendix 3: Interactive methods for your group

Here are some suggestions to help you make your sessions interactive. They are our own experience, on what we have learned and read and adapted as much as possible to our main aim, which is to promote the free exchange of ideas and arguments in group discussions about the faith. We are sure that with your creativity you will also be able to develop methods of your own.

1. Getting to know each other

Idea
Participants get to know each other better by using interesting statements.

How it works
1. Preparation: On a sheet of paper list ten (or more, depending on the size of your group) statements that say something about people. Include both simple and in-depth statements. For example:
   - I have a dog.
   - I enjoy singing.
   - I've been to three continents.
   - I've been baptized.
   - I hardly ever eat breakfast.
   - I doubt that God exists.
   - I like buying fair trade products.
   - I don't leave the house without makeup.
   - I've seen the pope in person.
   - I sometimes pray to Mary.

   Make a copy of this sheet for each group member.
2. Explain the rules: "We're going to play living bingo. You will be given a list of statements. The goal is to find a different person to match each statement within 15 minutes. Ask a person to choose a statement on your list that describes him. Have him write his name on your list beside the statement he chooses. Then move to another person. Each statement can be used only once."
3. Distribute pens and sheets. Have someone watch the time.
4. At the end of the game, discuss all the statements. For every statement, ask a participant to tell whose name he has noted and to tell briefly about his meeting that person.
5. Are people left unmentioned? Ask them to choose a statement that is applicable to them and briefly tell something about their relation to it.

Extra
Teens especially are stimulated by competition. You could give a small prize to the first person to find names for all ten statements.

Supplies
- sheets with statements
- pens
- a clock

2. Praying together

Idea
Group members become comfortable with praying together.

How it works
1. Tell the participants that you want to start off the evening by praying. If possible, go to the church or a chapel. Perhaps you can spend some time in front of the Blessed Sacrament. Otherwise you can place chairs near an icon.

Give participants a few minutes in silence to recollect themselves.

2. Give everyone a piece of paper and a pen. Ask them to write down an intention, something they would like to tell or ask God. For example, they may wish to pray for a person who is ill, for an exam to go well, or for refugees. Tell them that these will not be read by anyone else unless they allow it.
3. Collect the papers in a box.
4. Put the box in front of the altar or the Blessed Sacrament or before the icon.
5. Make the Sign of the Cross. As the group leader, introduce the prayer. You could start with: "Thank you, Lord, for bringing us together tonight. In this box are our prayers. Please hear them." Now tell the participants they are free to pray aloud the intentions they had written down.
6. When it has been silent for a few minutes after the last intention has been spoken aloud, end the prayer. You could end with: "Please hear these prayers of ours, Lord. Help us tonight to be respectful and attentive to each other. Help us to learn and to grow. Our Father ..." Make the Sign of the Cross.
7. Return to the original location to continue the session.

> **Supplies**
> - pieces of paper
> - pens
> - a box
> - preferably a church or chapel

3. Making groups

It can be conducive to the conversation to split the group into smaller ones. This way, participants who are less talkative will get more opportunities to speak. People will also share personal things more easily in a smaller group. We recommend small groups of three to five people. Experiment to see what works for your group.

A. Colored napkins

Idea
Groups are formed according to matching napkin colors.

How it works
1. Get as many colored napkins as there are people in your group, in as many colors as the number of groups you would like; for example, if you want three groups, you will need three colors. Be sure to have the same number of napkins of each color.
2. Use the napkins at the start of your activity, for example, with whatever food you might be serving (SEE B.4). Tell the group to keep their napkins because they'll need them later on.
3. When you are ready to break into small groups, ask the participants to take out their napkins. Ask them to locate the others in the room with the same color napkins as theirs. Then direct the small groups to areas where they can discuss the topic together.

> **Tips**
> A   You can steer the creation of small groups a little without participants noticing. Is there a shy teenager whose friend always does the talking? Give each of them a different color!
> B   You can come up with all sorts of variations; for example, substitute cups, straws, or name tags for napkins.
>
> **Supplies**
> - napkins of different colors

B. Shoes

Idea

Members are grouped according to shoes.

How it works

1. Ask all participants to take off one shoe and to lay it in a row with all the others. Don't tell them yet what the purpose is.
2. Divide the shoes into groups (decide beforehand how many groups you will have).
3. Now tell the members to put their shoes back on. The members whose shoes were grouped together will be in the same discussion group.

> **Supplies**
> • shoes of the participants

4. Warming up

Idea

Participants think and speak quickly off the top of their heads about the topic.

How it works

1. First, mention the topic of the session.
2. Tell the participants the activity is to get them thinking and sharing about the topic.
3. Explain the game: "I'm going to pass around a matchbox. You will each light a match in turns. As long as the match is burning you can spout whatever comes to your mind about the topic. Anything goes: opinions, questions, ideas, memories, and so on. When you must extinguish the match, you must stop talking and pass the matchbox to the next person."

4. Before you start the game, give everyone half a minute to reflect on the topic with his eyes closed. This is to prevent people from only copying what others say.
5. Select the first person to light a match, give him the matchbox, and tell him to start.
6. After the game, briefly summarize what has been said. Then resume the session.

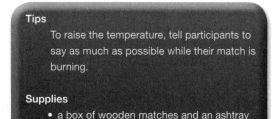

> **Tips**
> To raise the temperature, tell participants to say as much as possible while their match is burning.
>
> **Supplies**
> • a box of wooden matches and an ashtray

5. Processing the info

Idea

Every participant gets the task of listening extra closely to one particular person during this session, with the aim of listening to everyone with more attention.

How it works

1. Tell all participants to write their name on a separate piece of paper. Have them fold the notes so that the names are inside. Show them how you want them to fold the notes (e.g., twice) so that they are all folded in the same way.
2. Collect the papers in a bowl. Mix them up and give each participant one note. Tell participants they are not to receive their own name or the name of someone they know well. If someone has, collect the notes and hand them out again.

3. Once everyone has a name, say: "The person whose name you've received is the person you are going to give extra attention to during our conversations. Listen to this person extra closely, try to understand what he is saying, and ask him more questions. It's important to listen to everyone closely, but go the extra mile with this person."
4. Later in the session, remind members of this activity and encourage them to keep listening intently to and trying to understand the person whose name they received.

> **Supplies**
> - small pieces of paper, such as sticky notes
> - pens
> - bowl

6. Reflection

Idea
Every participant reflects on the session individually by answering three questions on paper.

How it works
1. List the following questions on a sheet of paper, and leave enough space for people to write their answers. Make enough copies for everyone in the group.
   a. What was new for me?
   b. What touched me? How did I feel? Happy, angry, afraid, sad? Why?
   c. What do I want to learn more about?
2. At the start of the moment of reflection, tell participants they will get five minutes to reflect on the evening using three questions.
3. Distribute sheets and pens and ask if anyone has any questions. If so, answer them.
4. Ask for silence and tell the group when to begin.

5. Should anyone have a question during the five minutes, answer it by whispering so as not to disturb others.
6. If needed, give some extra time.
7. When the time is up, encourage participants to take their answers home with them for further reflection and study. Tell them that they can find answers to many of their questions in the #TwGOD book and that they can ask any questions of the #TwGOD social media team, who would love to help them out.

> **Tips**
> You may end every session with these three questions. Buy a little notebook for each participant and ask him to bring it every time.
>
> **Supplies**
> - sheets of paper with questions
> - pens
> - clock

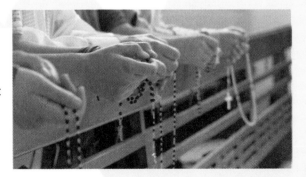

Receiving the Sacrament of Reconciliation can be a challenge, especially if you are not used to it – even if you are well prepared for it. Creating a cozy atmosphere in the place where priests will be hearing confessions helps people to find the courage they need to receive this sacrament. Have someone play the guitar and/or sing calm adoration hymns. Dim the lights, and place a large cross near the altar (if possible, well illuminated). Have the Blessed Sacrament exposed on the altar or in a side chapel. Have confessionals available or a pair of chairs, one for the priest and one for the penitent, beside an icon and candles. Have holy water, paper, and pens handy.

Opening hymn

Sign of the Cross, opening prayer

Scripture reading and a brief homily
- E.g., Isaiah 61:1–4; Luke 15:11–32; John 3:16–17; 2 Corinthians 5:18–21; Ephesians 1:3–10

Communal part: prayer for forgiveness
As the Our Father teaches us, we ask God for forgiveness:
- Good Father, we have sinned against you. We ask for forgiveness for everything we did wrong. R/. *Lord, have mercy on us.*
- Good God, you love us. You made us good, and yet we did the wrong thing. R/.
- Good Father, you want nothing more than that sinners return to you. Help us again and again to recognize your love. R/.
- Good Jesus, we are preparing to receive the Sacrament of Reconciliation. Help us, and forgive us our trespasses. R/.

Together we pray the Our Father.

Individual part: Sacrament of Reconciliation
Ultimately, life is all about our personal relationship with Jesus (SEE TWEETS 3.1 AND 4.1). As in any relationship, it is important to be honest, even about what went wrong and to ask forgiveness for all your sins. For that reason Jesus gave us the Sacrament of Reconciliation (Confession). He listens to you and forgives your sins through the priest (SEE TWEETS 3.38–3.39). As you are preparing for this, you can do several things in this church; if you have to choose, consider at least receiving the Sacrament of Reconciliation:
- Pray in front of the large cross placed in the church. Make the Sign of the Cross with holy water, remembering that in Baptism you became a child of God.
- Go and visit Jesus, present in the Blessed Sacrament, and speak to him (SEE TWEET 3.14).
- Write a letter to God or to a friend, asking for forgiveness. Place the letter in front of the large cross near the altar. Letters to God will be burned; other letters will be mailed.
- Go to the priest and receive the Sacrament of Reconciliation. Don't worry about how you should do this: the priest will help you.
- The priest will give you a candle. Light the candle in front of the altar and the cross, both symbols of Jesus, who sacrificed his life for you, and do your penance (SEE TWEET 3.38).

Hail Mary
A participant lights a candle before Mary's image. Then everyone prays the Hail Mary together.

Prayer of thanksgiving and blessing

Final hymn

Appendix 5: Prayers for the start and the end of the session

The best way to Tweet with God is through prayer. Praying in a group can be quite a challenge in the beginning. It is good to encourage the group members to pray from their heart. Especially in the beginning, you and they may need some help. Fortunately, the Church has a great tradition of beautiful prayers (SEE THE #TwGOD APP) that can be used. A short introduction, such as the one below, may help to integrate these into your sessions. Always start and conclude your prayer with the Sign of the Cross.

Opening prayers

Take, Lord …
Dear Lord, we come into your presence to thank you for this moment in which we may consider the greatness of your presence among us and the reasons why it is good to believe. We ask you to help us to think honestly about the faith and to recognize how everything comes together in your love. We want you, not us, to be the center of our lives and thoughts, and therefore we pray:

All: *Take, Lord, and receive all my liberty, my memory, my understanding, and my entire will, all I have and call my own. You have given all to me. To you, Lord, I return it. Everything is yours; do with it what you will. Give me only your love and your grace. That is enough for me.*

[SUSCIPE PRAYER OF ST. IGNATIUS]

Come, Holy Spirit …
Dear Lord, as we gather to think about you and your great gifts during this session, we ask you to be with us with your Holy Spirit. Together we pray:

All: *Come, Holy Spirit, Divine Creator, true source of light and fountain of wisdom! Pour forth your brilliance upon my dense intellect, dissipate the darkness which covers me, that of sin and of ignorance. Grant me a penetrating mind to under-stand, a retentive memory, method and ease in learning, the lucidity to comprehend, and abun-dant grace in expressing myself. Guide the begin-ning of my work, direct its progress, and bring it to successful completion. This I ask through Jesus*

Christ, true God and true man, living and reigning with you and the Father, forever and ever. Amen.

[STUDENT'S PRAYER OF ST. THOMAS AQUINAS]

Concluding prayers

Thank you, Lord …
Dear Lord, we thank you for our conversations, for what we learned about you and ourselves. Help us to make it part of our daily lives. Teach us to open ourselves to you. Holy Mary, Mother of Jesus, pray for us.

All: *Hail Mary …* (SEE TWEET 39).

Into your hands …
Thanking you for all we learned, we pray:

V/. Into your hands, Lord, I commend my spirit.
R/. *Into your hands, Lord, I commend my spirit.*
V/. You have redeemed us, Lord God of truth.
R/. *Into your hands, Lord, I commend my spirit.*
V/. Glory be to the Father, and to the Son, and to the Holy Spirit.
R/. *Into your hands, Lord, I commend my spirit.*

[PSALM 31:5; NIGHT PRAYER]

Praying with the Church
Always try to conclude your #TwGOD session in a church or chapel, possibly by praying the night prayer of the Church, Compline (SEE TWEET 3.13), or by a moment of adoration of the Blessed Sacra-ment (SEE TWEET 3.14). See www.tweetingwithgod.com/howto for sample prayers.

Appendix 6: A Confirmation course in Tweets

Depending on the age of the Confirmation group, you can either use the book and the app directly with the students or use only the online material and summarize for the students the items in the book (SEE C.2). In our view, at least the subjects listed below should be presented. The order in which you present them may change based on the questions of the group, but make sure you have covered them all in the end. Earlier we spoke about using #TwGOD in a group (SEE B.1–B.6). See also our suggestions for fun methods to work with groups (SEE APPENDIX 3). Here, the material is divided over 14 classes, as that seems to be the average duration of the preparation. If you can dedicate more time, you can divide the content of each class over two or more classes. The Tweets provide you with more than enough material.

How to read this table

Aim:	Here we indicate the main scope of this particular class.
Tweets:	The class is based on these Tweets.
Do:	This is a suggested activity for the group, apart from the faith discussion.
Pray:	Here we give a prayer suggestion.

(The "Do" and "Pray" sections contain examples that you can choose whether to follow.)

Preliminary preparations
Form a team, share your vision, make a plan, set a schedule (SEE ALSO APPENDIX 1).

Preparation meeting
- Meet the parents: they will want to know your plans; help them realize that they too need to learn about the faith (SEE C.4).
- Meet the participants: they need to get to know you and each other (SEE APPENDIX 3).

Class 1: God, Creation, and you
Aim:	See that you are a child of God: he loves you and is your Creator.
Tweets:	1.1, 1.2, 1.3, 1.5, 1.9, 4.1.
Do:	Make a drawing of you and God.
Pray:	Some songs, the Our Father, and the Hail Mary (learned by heart).

Class 2: Scripture and Tradition
Aim:	The Bible is more than just a book; God's revelation in Tradition.
Tweets:	1.6, 1.11, 1.10, 1.12, 1.15, 1.18.
Do:	Write on sticky notes the ways we know about God.
Pray:	Prayer with a psalm.

Team: Evaluation & team building

Class 3: Mary and the saints
Aim:	You're not alone: those in heaven pray with us!
Tweets:	1.38, 1.39, 1.40, 1.41, 4.15, 4.16.
Do:	Make your own rosary.
Pray:	A decade of the Rosary.

Class 4: Great Bible stories
Aim:	Get to know some chief events; see how they are related to Jesus.
Tweets:	1.22, 1.23, 1.24, 1.25.
Do:	Bring your Bible and make it a game to find the texts quickly.
Pray:	Prayer with a Bible text (SEE TWEET 3.8).

Class 5: Sin and evil
Aim: Realize how you are affected by the sin of our first parents.
Tweets: 1.4, 1.42, 1.34, 1.35, 1.36.
Do: Make drawings of sins (not necessarily yours); burn the drawings.
Pray: Adoration of the Blessed Sacrament: Jesus' love versus sin (SEE TWEETS 3.14 AND 4.13).

Class 6: Act
Volunteer at a nursing home, with the sisters of Mother Teresa, or for another charitable organization.

Class 7: God's great plan
Aim: Get to know the nucleus of our faith and what God saves us from.
Tweets: 1.26, 1.27, 1.28, 1.29.
Do: Invite a priest for at least this session and have a chat with him (SEE C.2).
Pray: Eucharistic adoration and blessing.

Team: Evaluation & team building

Class 8: Sacraments, liturgy, and prayer
Aim: The 7 sacraments; forms of prayer and liturgy.
Tweets: 3.35, 3.24, 3.1, 3.2, 3.3, 3.12, 3.14.
Do: Make lists of what you learn. Mark what you like and what you don't understand.
Pray: The Chaplet of Divine Mercy.

Class 9: Your own vocation
Aim: You too have a vocation; learn about how to find it.
Tweets: 3.50, 4.2, 4.3, 4.4, 4.5, 4.50.
Do: Make a drawing of yourself in 20 years' time.
Pray: Thanksgiving, spontaneous intercessory prayers by the participants.

Class 10: The Holy Spirit and Confirmation
Aim: The Holy Spirit is received in Baptism and Confirmation.
Tweets: 1.31, 1.32, 1.33, 3.36, 3.37, 3.34.
Do: Make a list of the gifts you ask from God at Confirmation; compare it with the gifts of the Spirit (SEE TWEET 1.32).
Pray: Prayer to the Holy Spirit (SEE TWEET 3.9).

Class 11: Forgiveness
Aim: You too need God's forgiveness; learn about grace and sin.
Tweets: 4.12, 4.13, 4.14, 3.38, 3.39.
Do: Write a letter to God, asking forgiveness, and prepare for Confession.
Pray: Pray the Rosary together.

Class 12: Pray
This is the right moment for receiving the Sacrament of Reconciliation (SEE APPENDIX 4).

Sacrament of Confirmation

Team: Evaluation

Class 13: Have fun
Have a celebration for all those who were confirmed. Possibly share pictures of the Confirmation, exchange experiences, and enjoy. Conclude with a short prayer of thanksgiving, during which Confirmation gifts can be blessed by the priest.

Class 14: Our faith summarized in the Creed
Write the Apostles' Creed on a board or a large sheet of paper. Let the class put a green dot next to the lines they like, a red dot next to the lines they do not like, and a yellow dot next to the lines they do not understand. That should give you ample material for discussion! Conclude, if possible, with thanksgiving and blessing with the Blessed Sacrament.

The authors would like to thank

Gino Anker, Anne Bakermans, Margreet Beenakker, Rowy van Dijk, Sasheeka Fernando, Fr. Henri ten Have, Mark Heins, Gerard van der Klein, Rev. Fr. Stephan Kuik, Daria Maroń-Ptak, Edith Peters, Barbara Schoo, Lidwine Tax, Lodewijk Tax, Ashley Tax-Nijhof, Annemarie Scheerboom, Fr. Grzegorz Zakrzewski, and Marian van Zutven-Van Kampen. Many thanks to Fr. Johannes van Voorst tot Voorst in the Netherlands and Raluca Cocuţ in Romania, as well as to the youngsters with whom they tested this manual.